The Guitar Of Doc Watson

MW00574547

Editor: Aaron Stang
Transcribed by Fred Sokolow
Transcriptions Edited by Tod Edmondson
Cover Design: Joann Carrera
Photos Courtesy of Manny Greenhill

Alfred Publishing Co., Inc.
16320 Roscoe Blvd., Suite 100
P.O. Box 10003
Van Nuys, CA 91410-0003
alfred.com

ISBN-10: 0-7692-1784-2
ISBN-13: 978-0-7692-1784-0

Contents

$\mathcal{D}oc\ \mathcal{W}atson$: *A BIOGRAPHY*

A generation of flatpicking guitarists such as Tony Rice, Norman Blake and Dan Crary owe a great debt to Doc Watson. In the early '60s, he raised the expectations of the aspiring acoustic guitarist and transformed the flat-top guitar from a rhythm to a lead instrument that could be as dazzling as a fiddle, banjo or mandolin. Perhaps more importantly, Doc Watson is an authentic, living purveyor of traditional musical forms more commonly found on old, re-issued 78s! He breathes life into the old string band music and country blues of the '20s and '30s, and combines these forms with more urban contemporary country, swing, rockabilly and pop music. Somehow the essence of the older music comes through.

Born Arthel Watson on March 3, 1923 in Deep Gap, North Carolina, he was blinded in his infancy. Several generations of Watsons had lived in this area which was rich with the music of the region, and Doc grew up listening to hymns, ballads and down home string band music by the likes of Gid Tanner, Charlie Poole and Riley Puckett. He played many instruments as a child and started on guitar at age thirteen. By his teens he was playing solo and with his brother on local radio shows. He got the nickname "Doc" in '42 while playing on one such program. It was suggested by a member of the audience when the emcee wanted a more pronounceable name than Arthel for his introduction.

Besides listening to the Carter Family, Jimmie Rodgers, the Delmore Brothers and other hillbilly string band music, Doc heard all the music of his time: the country blues of fingerpickers like Mississippi John Hurt, the more urban country/jazz fingerpicking of Merle Travis and Chet Atkins, western swing, rockabilly, urban country western, and pop. Doc was married and had two children in '54 when he and pianist Jack Williams formed a honky tonk dance band. Called Jack Williams and the Country Gentlemen, they played rockabilly, country western, pop standards and square dance tunes in the honky tonks and VFW clubs of East Tennessee and Western North Carolina. Doc's guitar was a '53 Les Paul electric. To fill occasional square dance requests, he learned to flatpick fiddle tunes on the guitar, as Joe Maphis had done in the mid '30s.

Doc played with Jack Williams throughout the '50s, but never stopped playing traditional mountain music with his family and friends at home, including banjoist Clarence Ashley and Doc's father in law, Gaither Carlton. In 1960, Ralph Rinzler (once mandolin player for one of the first Northern bluegrass groups, The Greenbriar Boys) came to Deep Gap to record Clarence Ashley. Doc was "discovered." Within a few years he was playing for enthusiastic audiences at folk festivals and college concerts and was recording Lps for Vanguard Records. His proficiency on the guitar amazed other acoustic guitarists and he was uniquely gifted at communicating traditional music to city audiences.

In 1964, Doc was joined on recordings and tours by his son Merle, who was named after fingerpicking guitarist Merle Travis (as you can hear Doc tell Travis on the Nitty Gritty Dirt Band's *Will The Circle Be Unbroken* recording). At age fifteen, Merle had taught himself to play guitar while Doc was on the road! More than an accompanist, Merle was Doc's road manager and guide, and he contributed original songs, played "twin guitar" harmonies to Doc's flatpicked fiddle tunes, and developed a unique open tuning slide guitar style. For twenty years the father and son enjoyed a relationship that was musically inspiring for both of them.

Merle's death in a tractor accident on his farm in 1985 was a great loss. Doc still occasionally performs and records. With over three dozen recordings and three decades of touring behind him, he has brought traditional American music to audiences who otherwise might never hear the "real thing." His warmth as a singer and storyteller, as well as his musical expertise, have helped preserve a very valuable part of our heritage: the traditional music of the South.

Doc Watson's Guitar Style

Flatpicking

Watson plays a Gallagher guitar, though he made his first records with a Martin, and uses medium gauge strings and a fairly stiff nylon flatpick. He says that 75% of his picking motion comes from his arm, the other 25% from his wrist.

He almost always plays downstrokes on the downbeats and upstrokes on the upbeats, so those fast fills and fiddle tunes are made of alternating down- and upstrokes. This even applies to "crosspicking," as in this example from *Beaumont Rag:*

Doc favors the keys of G and C for flatpicking melodies, and he often capos up a few frets for this reason. For instance, *Black Mountain Rag* is played in the keys of D and A, so Doc capos up two frets so that he can solo in the C and G positions. He recommends that you practice your first position C and G major scales to play his type of fills and fiddle tune melodies:

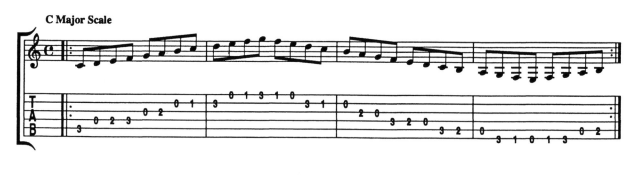

When he backs up his voice or another instrument, Doc flatpicks Carter-style accompaniment: Pick down on the bass note that is the root of your chord, then brush down and up on the treble strings; then pick down on the bass note that is the fifth of your chord and brush down and up on the treble strings. Occasionally, connect the chords with bass runs:

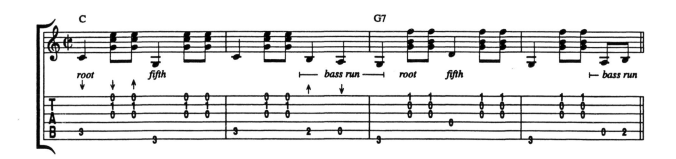

You will find hundreds of variations of this basic Carter lick when you study Doc's accompaniment to vocal tunes like 'Rangement Blues and Blue Ridge Mountain Blues, or Merle's accompaniment in the Double File/Salt Creek medley. Also notice the many tasty fills Doc adds when there is a pause in his vocal line. Sometimes in a fast tune, the Carter lick is simplified so that there are fewer brush strokes on the treble strings. In a slower or funkier rhythmic feel, there may be more brush strokes added:

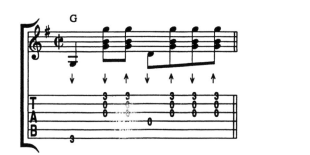
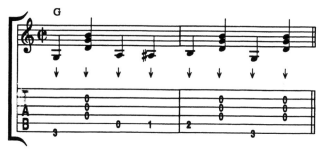

Some of Doc's faster tunes have a "Texas swing-style" accompaniment in which the backup player picks downstrokes and damps (mutes) the chords. You can mute the strings with your left hand by raising the fretting fingers after strumming a chord, so that they touch, but do not fret, the strings. This is easily done with movable chords, i.e. chords that have no open strings. With first position chords which do include open strings, you can damp a strummed chord with the base of the palm of your picking hand. Cotton-Eyed Joe contains some swing style accompaniment:

Fingerpicking

When Doc fingerpicks, his little finger is usually lightly touching the pickguard for stability. He uses a thumbpick and one fingerpick, as he uses his index finger but not his middle finger to pick treble strings. However, many of his arrangements are easier to play if you use your thumb, index and middle fingers!

Doc fingerpicks in the Merle Travis style, meaning he plays an alternating bass accompaniment with his thumb, usually alternating the root and fifth of the chord being played. This thumb/bass rock steady rhythm is augmented by notes picked on the treble string by the index finger. These can be melody notes or rhythmic fill. Sometimes the alternate bass notes (on beats two and four) are brush strokes, and two or three strings are sounded:

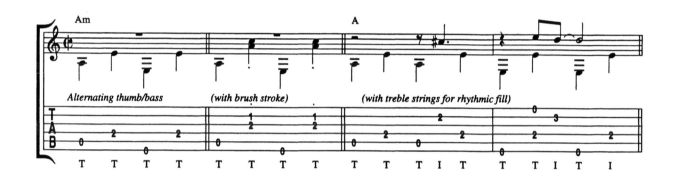

For good examples of fingerpicked melody, see *You Must Come In At The Door, Deep River Blues, Windy And Warm* and *Doc's Guitar*. Also see Merle's fingerpicked open-tuning solos in *Bonaparte's Retreat, Florida Blues* and *'Rangement Blues*.

Like Merle Travis, Doc often damps his bass strings when fingerpicking by lightly touching them with the fleshy lower palm of his picking hand. Another Travis technique he employs is wrapping his left thumb around the back of the guitar neck to fret the 6th string. It's a short cut to barring certain chords. Doc does it, but he doesn't recommend it to other guitarists!

A Final Word

Whether fingerpicking or flatpicking, nobody has a better rhythmic swing than Doc Watson. It's not a result of some unusual, secret technique. The only way to pick up some of that rhythmic feel is to listen to and play along with Doc's recordings. In fact, studying these transcriptions and listening to and playing along with Doc is one of the best things an acoustic guitarist can do to develop chops and good taste!

Good luck,
Fred Sokolow

Performance Notes

BEAUMONT RAG

Doc learned this instrumental in the '30s from radio broadcasts on XERA the powerful Del Rio station on the Texas/Mexico border. It was first recorded in '26 by Smith's Garage Fiddle Band on Vocalion Records. This transcription is from Doc's second Vanguard Lp, *Doc Watson and Son*, recorded in '65 (VRS 9170). It was re-released on the Ranwood CD, *The Essential Doc Watson* (VCD 4546). Doc also recorded a version of the tune with Chet Atkins on their *Reflections* album.

On this early version he played 12-string and did some fancy crosspicking in the second section. Merle provided basic flatpicking backup. It's a flashy showcase for Doc's fast flatpicking style.

BLACK MOUNTAIN RAG

This is one of the first fiddle tunes Doc worked up in his famous flatpicking style. It dazzled audiences in the '60s and became his signature tune. He first heard the popular fiddle piece played by Leslie Keith and the Stanley Brothers who had a daily radio broadcast on radio WCYB, Bristol, Virginia-Tennessee.

This version is from the '83 *Doc And Merle Watson's Guitar Album on Flying Fish* (FF 301). It's similar to his '60s arrangement, but halfway through there is a key change from D to A. Doc had fiddler Mark O'Connor use an open A tuning on this section for a more authentic sound. Doc ends the tune with some bluesy improvisation on the guitar.

To get those false harmonics in Section III, Doc pinches the flatpick so that the edge of his thumb and the pick touch the strings when he brushes down.

BLUE RIDGE MOUNTAIN BLUES

At least eight generations of Watsons have lived in the Blue Ridge in North Carolina. Doc first heard this tune in '29 or '30 on a Riley Puckett "78" that came with his family's first wind-up Victrola. It has become a bluegrass standard, recorded by Bill Monroe, Jim and Jesse and others. Doc's three solos illustrate his ability to embellish a tune without losing its original melody. He also plays several typical Watson "fills" during pauses in his vocal.

The transcription is from the '85 Doc And Merle Watson *Pickin' The Blues* album on Flying Fish (FF 352). Merle's backup is in the swing-like "damped chord" style described in the Introduction.

BONAPARTE'S RETREAT

This old bagpipe tune has long been a favorite of fiddlers and banjoists in the Southern string band tradition. Merle arranged and fingerpicked lead on this guitar version from the '73 Poppy album *Then And Now* (PP-LA022-F). Besides Doc's backup, there are Dobro solos and accompaniment from the fine guitarist, Norman Blake.

COTTON-EYED JOE

This old American dance tune appears here as a twin-guitar piece, with Doc and Merle harmonizing in the flatpicking fiddle-tune style. A third guitar plays swing-style "damped chord" accompaniment. The tune appeared on the Sugar Hill album Down South, recorded in '84 (SH 3742) with Sam Bush helping out on fiddle.

DEEP RIVER BLUES

Doc learned to play this Delmore Brothers tune when he was sixteen, and around 1960 he worked out the brilliant fingerpicking version that became one of his signature tunes. It appeared as transcribed here, on his first Vanguard Lp in '64 *(Doc Watson* VRS-9152) and is now available on a Ranwood album with the same title (VMD 79152).

DOC'S GUITAR
Doc recorded this speedy, original fingerpicking instrumental on his first Vanguard Lp. The same version, transcribed below, is now on the Ranwood, *Doc Watson* album, VMD 79152.

DOUBLE FILE/SALT CREEK
This medley of fiddle tunes, recorded in '75 on United Artists' *Doc Watson - Memories* album (UA, LA 423-H2), is a flatpicking showcase for Doc. It also features some typical flatpicking backup from Merle and ends with a twin-guitar father/son duet.

FLORIDA BLUES
This old fiddle tune gets a flatpick treatment from Doc and a slide guitar rendering from Merle. Merle tuned his guitar to open G, though the song is played in the key of D. The tune appeared on the '78 United Artists' *Look Away* album, UA LA 887-H.

LIFE IS LIKE A RIVER
Doc wrote this philosophical gospel tune. It appears on the '91 Sugar Hill recording *My Dear Old Southern Home* (SH-C-3795). Doc's fingerpicking is supported by Jack Lawrence's Carter-style backup guitar.

NASHVILLE PICKIN'
Doc recorded this flatpicking tour-de-force instrumental on his '66 *Southbound* Lp, which is now available from Ranwood (VMD OR CV 79213). John Pilla played backup guitar in first position.

'RANGEMENT BLUES
From the United Artists' *Look Away* album (UA LA 887-H). Merle played open-G tuning slide guitar and Doc flatpicked backup with a few of his characteristic fills. The chorus of this twelve-bar blues is the same as the last verse of Blind Lemon Jefferson's tune, *Matchbox,* recorded in the '20s.

THOUGHTS OF NEVER
Merle recorded this original classic guitar piece with piano accompaniment on the '75 Memories album (United Artists UA LA423-H2). In the liner notes, Doc said, "Because it is so expressive in the mood it sets, this is one of the most beautiful tunes I have ever heard. It was composed by my son Merle."

WINDY AND WARM
Doc learned this John D. Loudermilk instrumental from an early '60s Chet Atkins Lp that included Boots Randolph and Floyd Cramer. He has recorded it many times. The tight-harmony twin guitar version transcribed below comes from the '85 Flying Fish, *Doc And Merle Watson Pickin' The Blues* album, FF 352.

YOU MUST COME IN A THE DOOR
Doc added some original lyrics to this traditional gospel song when he recorded his *On Praying Ground* album in '90 for Sugar Hill (SH C or CD 3779). Jack Lawrence added some fingerpicking accompaniment.

LIFE IS LIKE A RIVER
Doc wrote this philosophical gospel tune. It appears on the '91 Sugar Hill recording *"My Dear Old Southern Home"* (SH-C-3795). Doc's fingerpicking is supported by Jack Lawrence's Carter-style backup guitar.

Beaumont Rag

By DOC WATSON

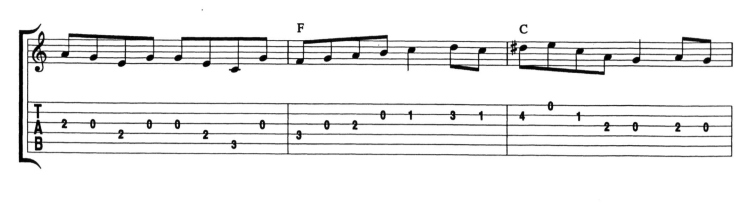

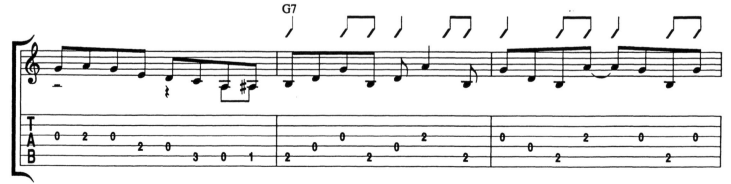

Beaumont Rag – 3 – 3
P0974GTX

Black Mountain Rag

By DOC WATSON

Fast 2-beat ♩ = 120

Capo on 2nd fret (actual key: D)

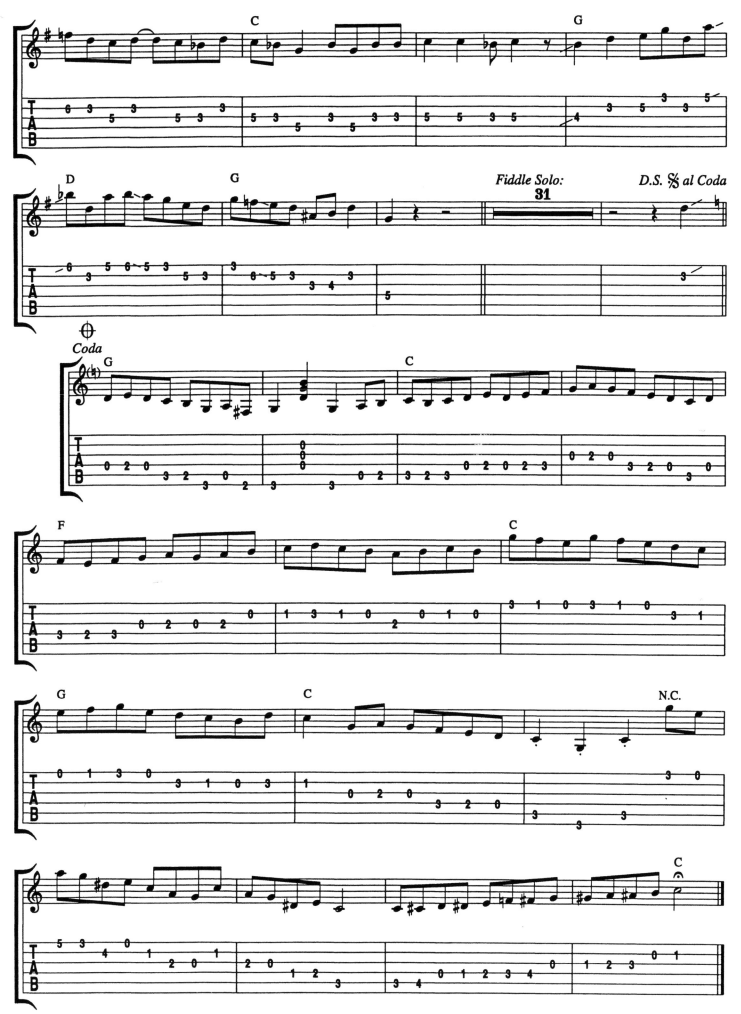

Blue Ridge Mountain Blues

Moderate country shuffle ♩ = 100
Capo on 4th fret (actual key: E)

By DOC WATSON

Blue Ridge Mountain Blues -- 5 - 2
P0974GTX

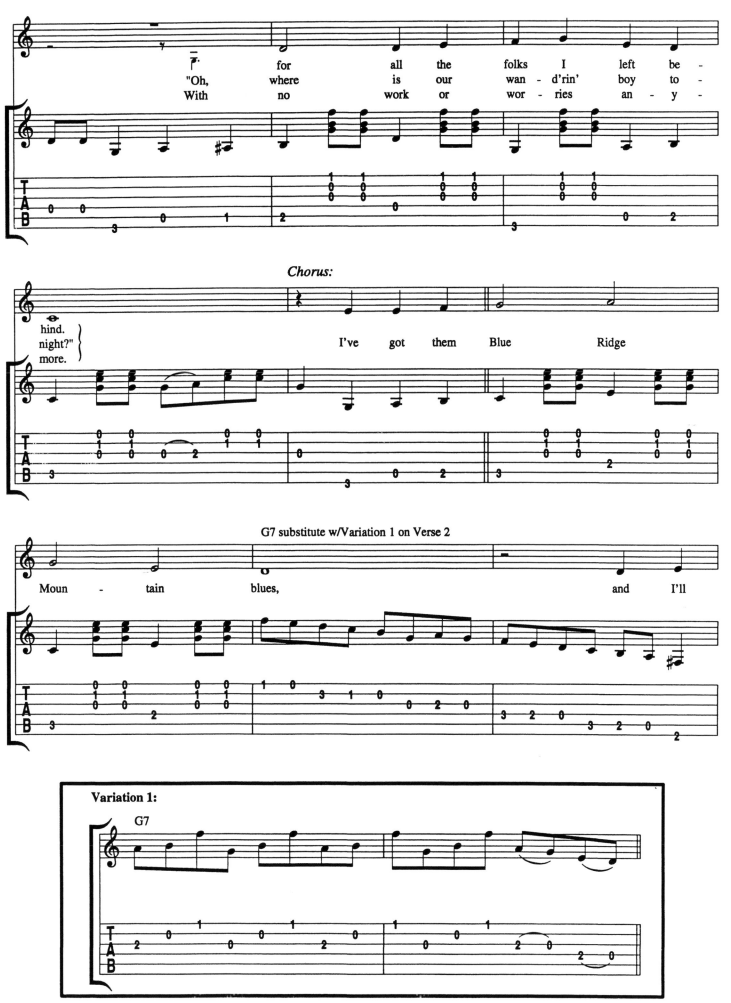

20

stand   right   here   and   say:

"My grip is packed   to   trav-el, { I'll / soon } be scratch - in'

gra - vel   for   that Blue Ridge   far   a - way."

way."   way."

Bonaparte's Retreat

By DOC WATSON

22

Bonaparte's Retreat – 3 – 2
P0974GTX

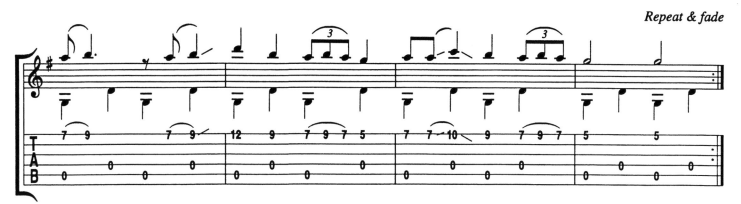

Bonaparte's Retreat – 3 – 3

P0974GTX

Cotton-Eyed Joe

By DOC WATSON

Copyright © 1984 HILLGREEN MUSIC (BMI)
International Copyright Secured   Made In U.S.A.   All Rights Reserved

Guitar & Fiddle Solo: (2nd time Rhy. Gtr. only)

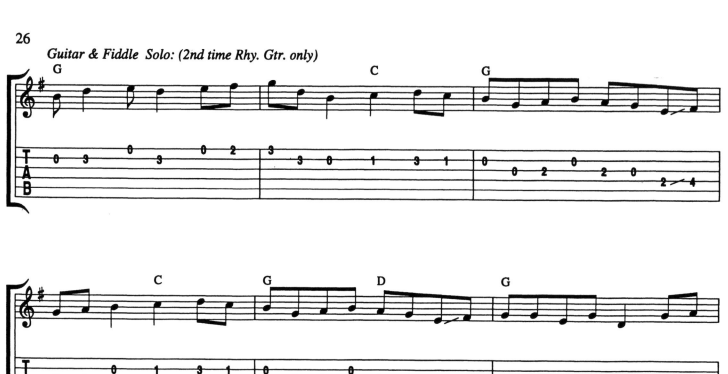

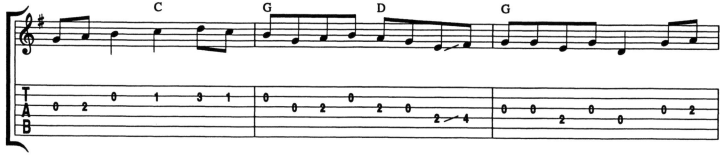

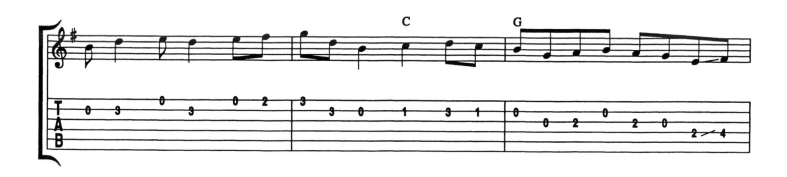

long time a-go.

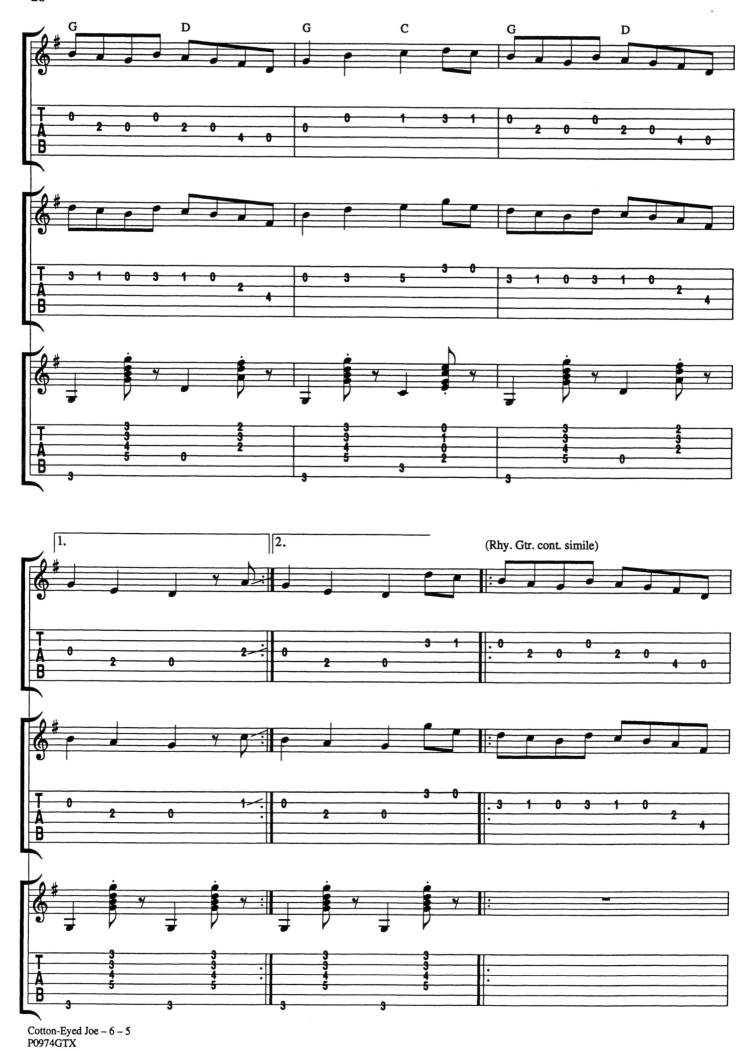

Cotton-Eyed Joe – 6 – 5
P0974GTX

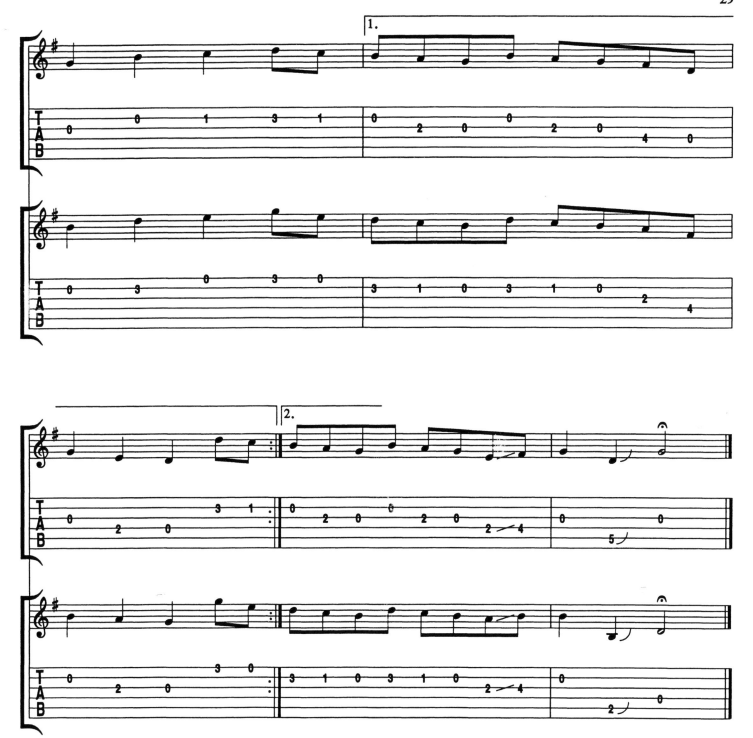

Verse 2:
Down in the cotton patch, down below,
Ev'rybody's singin' the Cotton-Eyed Joe,
Ev'rybody's singin' 'bout Cotton-Eyed Joe.
Had not've been for the Cotton-Eyed Joe,
I'd-'ve been married a long time ago,
I'd-'ve been married a long time ago.
(To Solo:)

Verse 3:
Tune my fiddle and rosin my bow;
Gonna make music ev'rywhere I go,
Play a little tune called Cotton-Eyed Joe.
Had not've been for the Cotton-Eyed Joe,
I'd-'ve been married a long time ago.
I'd-'ve been married a long time ago.
(To Coda)

Deep River Blues

By DOC WATSON

Moderate two-beat ♩ = 90
Capo on 1st fret (actual key: F)

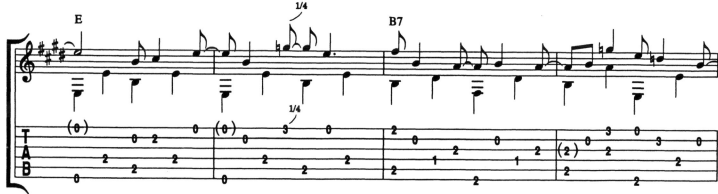

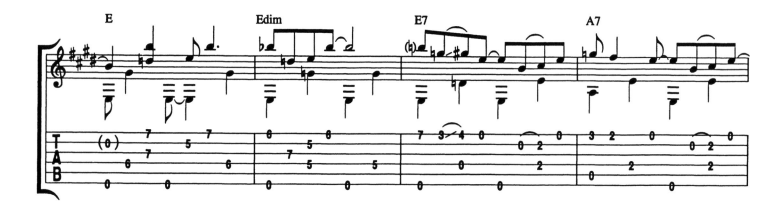

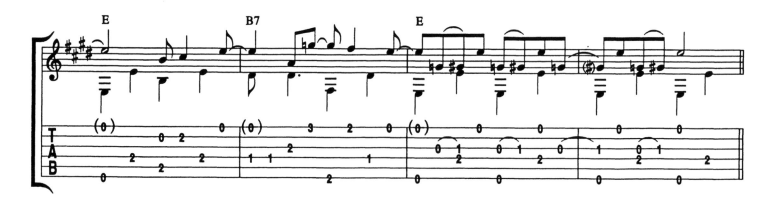

Deep River Blues – 4 – 1
P0974GTX

got ___ them   deep   riv - er   blues. ___
got ___ them   deep   riv - er   blues. ___
got ___ them   deep   riv - er   blues. ___

Doc's Guitar

By DOC WATSON

* Capo on 3rd fret (actual key: E♭)

substitute w/Variation 1, 2nd time

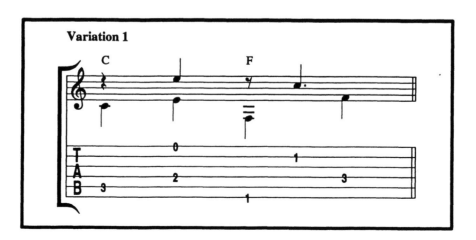

Variation 1

Doc's Guitar – 3 – 1
P0974GTX

substitute w/Variation 2, 2nd time

Doc's Guitar – 3 – 2
P0974GTX

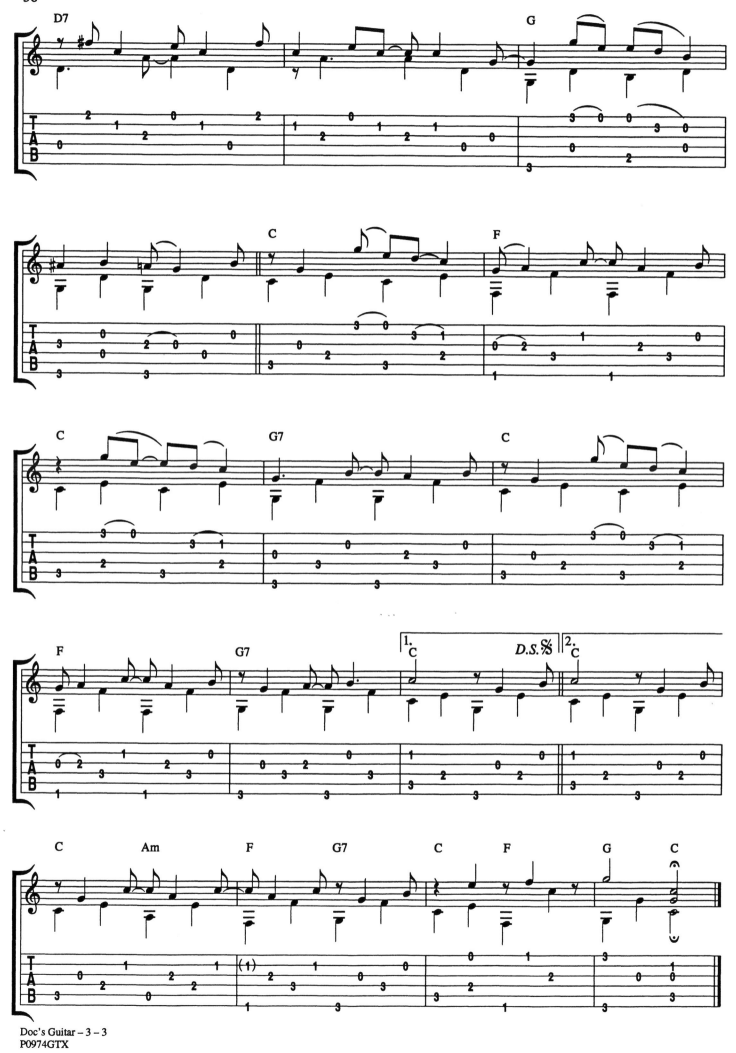

Double File/Salt Creek

By DOC WATSON

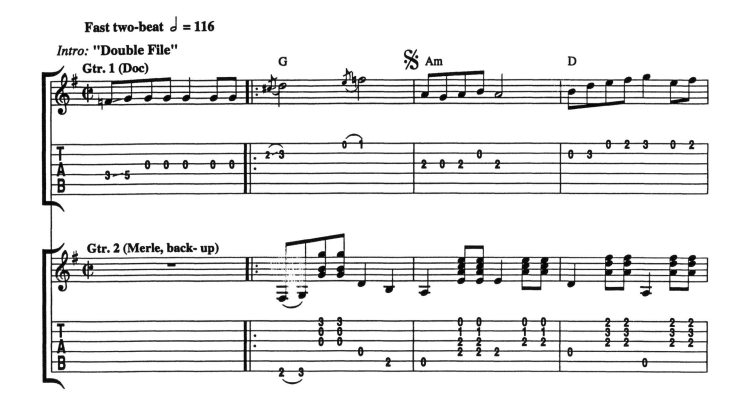

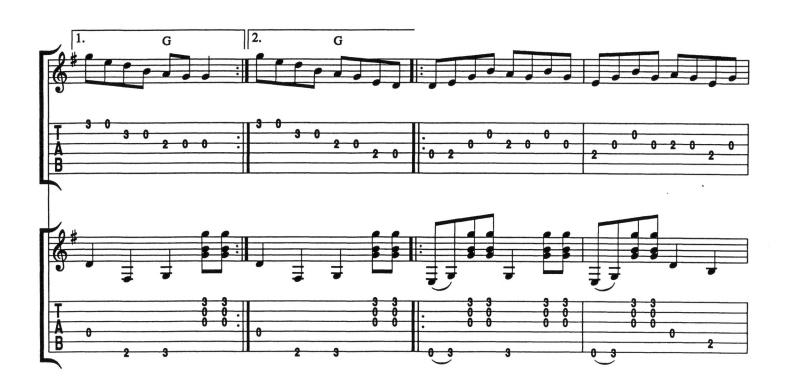

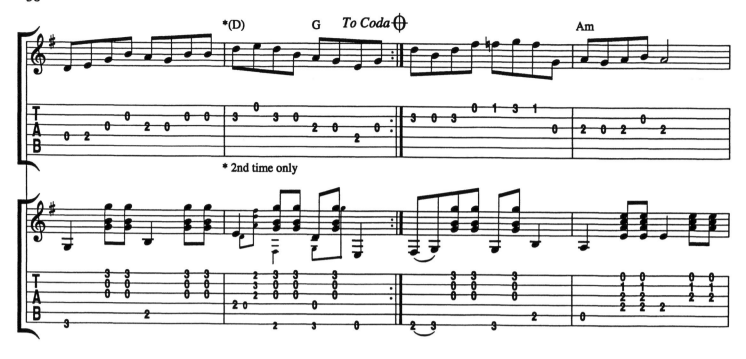

* 2nd time only

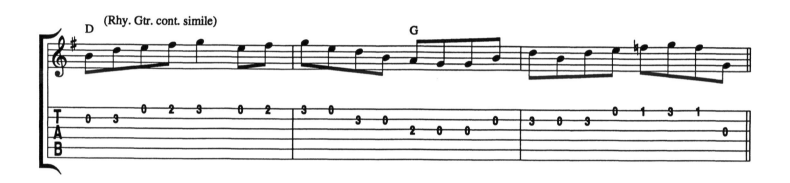

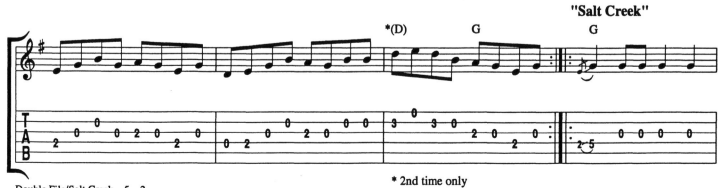

* 2nd time only

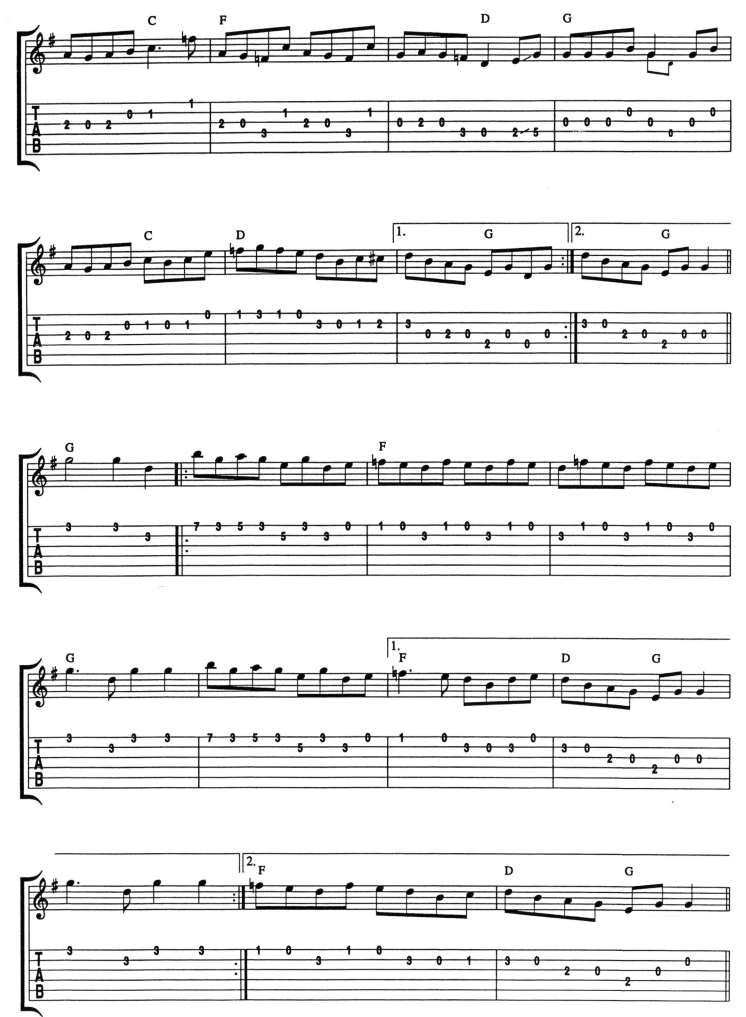

"Salt Creek" *("Twin Guitars")*

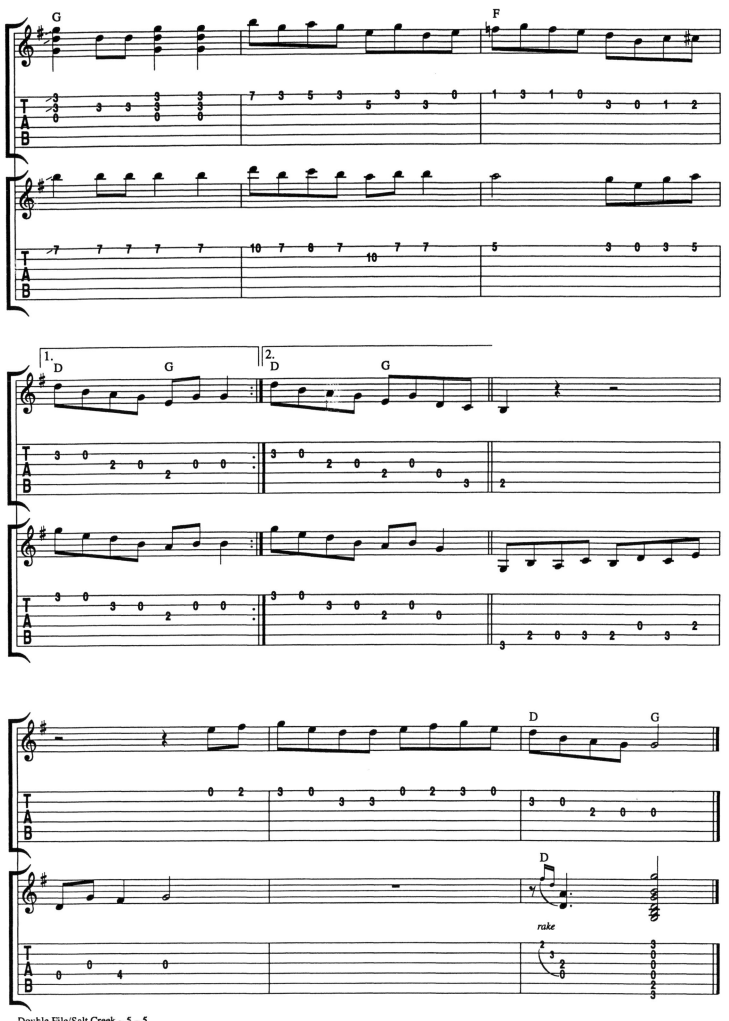

Double File/Salt Creek – 5 – 5
P0974CTX

Florida Blues

By DOC WATSON

Moderate country two - beat ♩ = 117

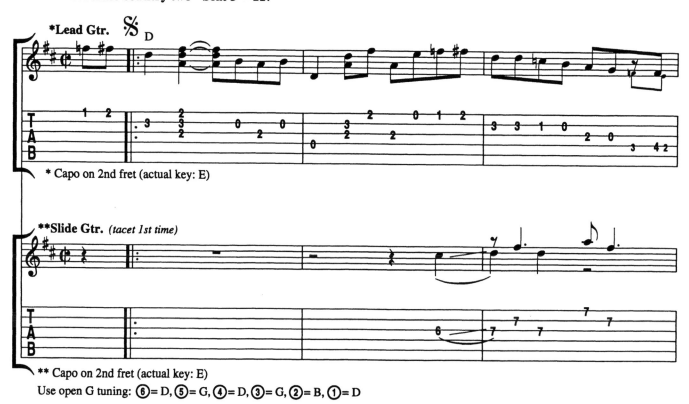

* Capo on 2nd fret (actual key: E)

Slide Gtr. (tacet 1st time)

** Capo on 2nd fret (actual key: E)
Use open G tuning: ⑥= D, ⑤= G, ④= D, ③= G, ②= B, ①= D

Florida Blues – 4 – 1
P0974GTX

Gtr. *(back-up for fiddle solo) (Slide Gtr. cont. simile)*

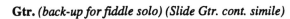

Slide Gtr. Solo: (back-up cont. simile)

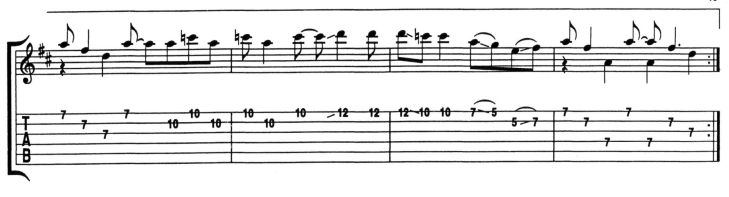

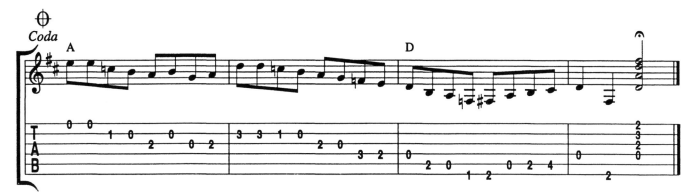

Florida Blues – 4 – 4
P0974GTX

Life Is Like A River

By DOC WATSON

Moderate country two - beat ♩ = 86
Capo third fret (actual key = Cm)

Am
⑤ A
⑥ E
(cont. simile)

Dm

Am   Dm   E7   F   Am

Verse:
Am

1. Life is like a riv - er _____ that runs to e - ter - ni - ty, and
(2.) dark and mud - dy cur - rent that can sweep your boat _ from sight. If you
rode this rag - ing riv - er _____ when the banks were cav - in' in. When the

Dm

Am   Dm   E7   F   Am

all must ride that riv - er, hon - ey, just like you and me. ___ It's
pass that point of no re - turn, there's a dark and end - less night. _ There's
storms have al - most beat - en us, we've al - ways tried a - gain. ___ Let's

Life Is Like a River – 3 – 2
P0974GTX

52

Nashville Pickin'

By DOC WATSON

substitute w/Variation 2, 2nd time

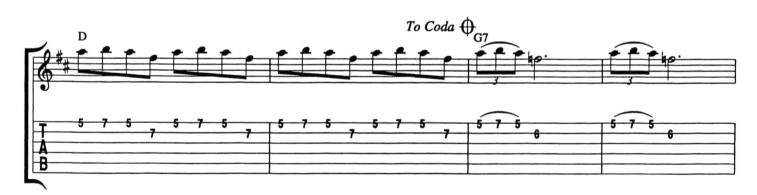

Variation 2

'Rangement Blues

By DOC WATSON

Bright two-beat ♩ = 115

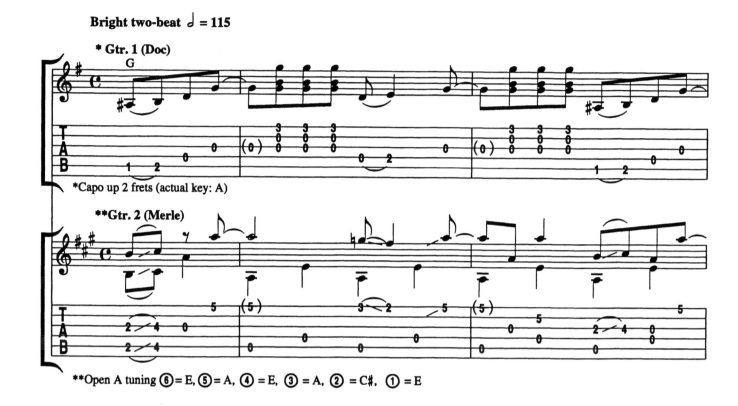

*Capo up 2 frets (actual key: A)

**Gtr. 2 (Merle)

**Open A tuning ⑥ = E, ⑤ = A, ④ = E, ③ = A, ② = C♯, ① = E

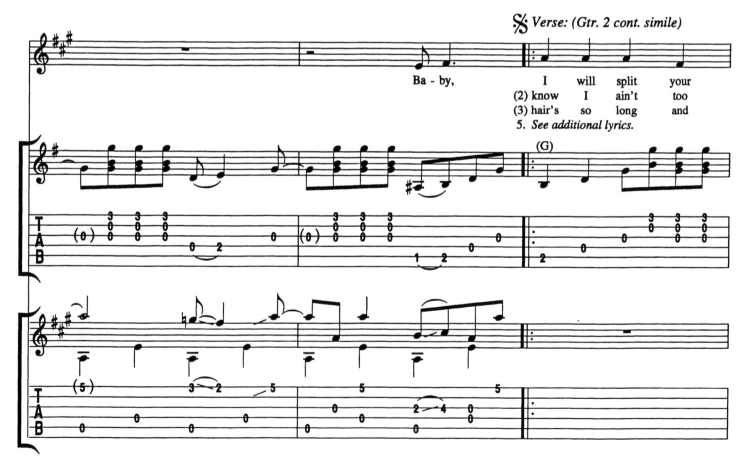

Verse: (Gtr. 2 cont. simile)

Ba - by,   I   will   split   your

(2) know   I   ain't   too

(3) hair's   so   long   and

5. *See additional lyrics.*

4. *Slide guitar solo (Verse and Chorus)*

5. I will be a good provider, honey, I ain't gonna fail.
   I got no other women tied to my coat-tail, mama.

   (To Chorus:)

Windy And Warm

By JOHN C. LOUDERMILK

Moderate two-beat $\quad \downharpoonright = 87$

Both Gtrs. capo on 3rd fret (actual key: Cm)

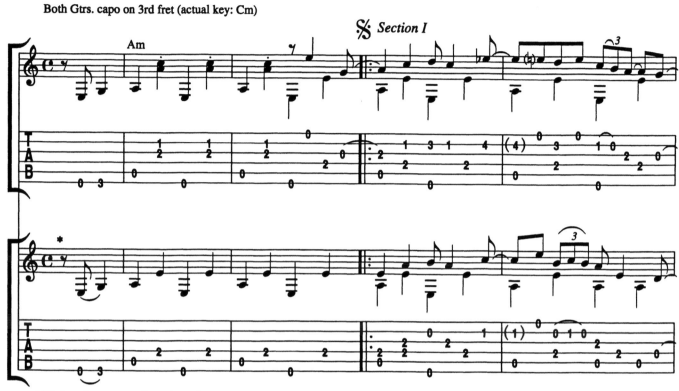

*Slight palm mute on bass throughout tune.

Windy And Warm – 6 – 1
P0974GTX

Windy And Warm – 6 – 2
P0974GTX

64

Windy And Warm – 6 – 3
P0974GTX

66

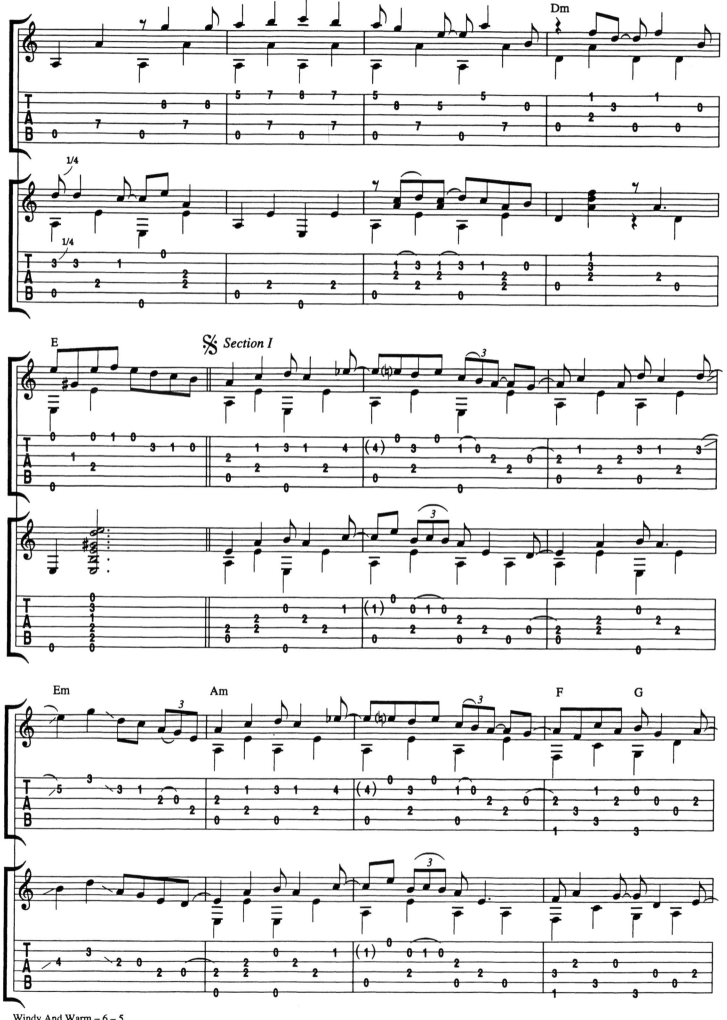

Windy And Warm – 6 – 5
P0974GTX

Section IV

Thoughts Of Never

By MERLE WATSON

You Must Come In At The Door

By DOC WATSON

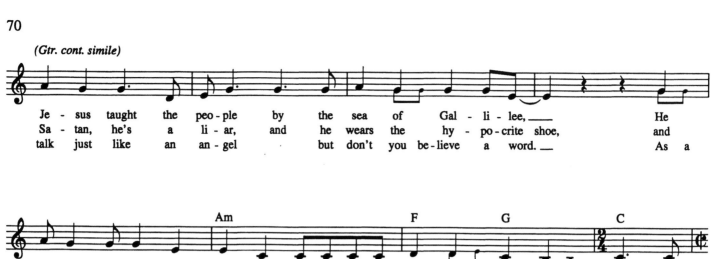

Je - sus taught the peo - ple by the sea of Gal - li - lee, ___ He
Sa - tan, he's a li - ar, and he wears the hy - po - crite shoe, and
talk just like an an - gel but don't you be - lieve a word. ___ As a

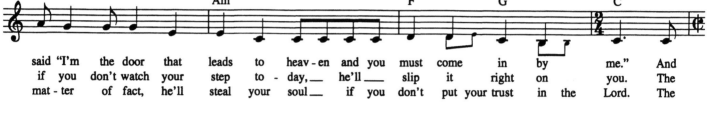

Am   F   G   C

said "I'm the door that leads to heav - en and you must come in by me." And
if you don't watch your step to - day, ___ he'll ___ slip it right on you. The
mat - ter of fact, he'll steal your soul ___ if you don't put your trust in the Lord. The

Chorus:

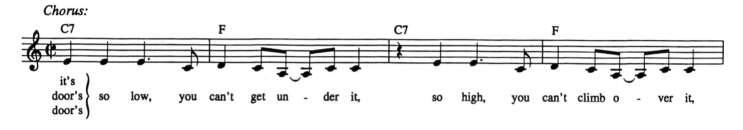

C7   F   C7   F

it's
door's } so low, you can't get un - der it, so high, you can't climb o - ver it,
door's }

To Coda ⊕

C7   F   G

so wide, ___ you'll nev - er get a - round it. You must come in at the

Gtr. Solo: (2nd time Fiddle Solo: Gtr. plays back - up)

door.

You Must Come In At The Door - 3 - 2
P0974GTX

You Must Come In At The Door – 3 – 3
P0974GTX